MASTERS OF WORLD PAINTING

Rubens

AURORA ART PUBLISHERS · LENINGRAD

COMPILED AND INTRODUCED BY VERA RAZDOLSKAYA
TRANSLATED FROM THE RUSSIAN BY NATALIA JOHNSTONE
DESIGNED BY VIACHESLAV BAKHTIN

P $\frac{4903020000\text{-}145}{023(01)\text{-}83}$ без объявления

The name of Rubens brings to mind at once a great number of paintings imbued with a profound feeling for life, rich and dynamic, radiating a wealth of colour. The work of this outstanding master has become synonymous with an art of striking emotional power and vitality, of tremendous passion and heroic endeavour. No other Flemish artist so clearly embodied in his paintings the spiritual upsurge of this small nation, full of creative force, at a time when it was experiencing one of the most eventful and glorious periods in its history. The best features of Flanders' national culture were fully expressed in Rubens' art. He established the path of development and the basic artistic principles of the Flemish school. Indeed, the influence of his powerful genius can be seen in the work of every representative artist of this school.

Rubens' life and his career were distinguished by remarkably good fortune. He enjoyed recognition early, and throughout his artistic development he experienced no setbacks or failures. Endowed with unusual strength of imagination and an original vision of life, he created his whole world of images and forms. He could say of himself: "My talent is such that no undertaking, however vast in size or diversified in subject, has ever surpassed my courage."

Peter Paul Rubens was born in 1577. His artistic idiom was formed during one of the most interesting and complex periods in the history of European art, when the main principles of Mannerism had already become outdated and new and varied artistic conceptions were being established. While he was studying at Antwerp, Rubens encountered various trends in the artistic life of the Netherlands. His first teachers, Tobias Verhaecht and Adam van Noort, had ties with the realistic traditions of the art of the Netherlands; the work of his third teacher, Otto van Veen, tended toward the Italian Romanists. Later, in Italy, Rubens had a chance not only to study thoroughly the heritage of antiquity and the Renaissance, but also to imbibe those aesthetic views which, at the turn of the century, found their most articulate expression in the art of his older Italian contemporaries, Caravaggio and Annibale Carracci. Rubens was deeply influenced by Caravaggio's daring realism, but he was also attracted by Renaissance traditions and

the reflection of these in the paintings of Annibale Carracci, which also showed early features of Baroque. Rubens developed the achievements of these masters in his own artistic exploration, which belonged wholly to the art of the new century.

Among the eminent painters who abounded in the seventeenth century, Rubens stands out not so much for his exceptional skill — Rembrandt, Velázquez, Hals, and Poussin were equally outstanding in this respect—as for his striking versatility. No one else, perhaps, embodied so vividly and completely the complex range of artistic trends in that brilliant epoch.

Rubens, certainly one of the greatest masters of realism, is closely linked with the popular traditions of the Netherlands. At the same time he is a brilliant representative, one of the founders, we may say, of Baroque art. His genius fused this heterogeneity into an absolutely integral and profoundly original style, but he did not acquire this style overnight. His first important works were painted in Italy, at which time he was not yet free of influence; his art matured only after he returned to Antwerp in 1608, when he came in touch with the life of his country.

His enormous gift as a decorative painter and the exceptional power of his imagination made Rubens a master of monumental composition, the creator of great decorative cycles which were splendid embellishments for Baroque churches and palaces. At the same time his faultless handling of decor and his admirable ability to create emotive gestures are combined with a lively and powerful feeling for whatever he depicted. However boundless the flight of his fancy, he never lost contact with reality, and the most allegorical of themes received full expression in his work.

An artist full of vitality, Rubens perceived life sensually and spontaneously. All his means of artistic expression, used with disciplined logic as well as with utmost boldness and freedom, serve to convey the sensual aspect of the subject matter. Early in life Rubens achieved very high technical perfection. He was a superb draughtsman and displayed inexhaustible inventiveness in composition. But first and foremost he always remained a painter. It is his colour, rich, sonorous, and saturated, that expresses his fertile vision of the world.

The distinctive features of Rubens' art were already manifest in the first altarpieces he produced after his return from Italy: the large triptych of the *Raising of the Cross* (1610—11, now in Antwerp Cathedral), with its tense, pathetic composition built on very daring contrasts; and the second triptych, only slightly less large, the *Descent from the Cross*, where stormy dynamism gives way to a solution of calmer balance (1612, Antwerp Cathedral; plates 1 and 2 show a version of the central panel in the Hermitage, Leningrad). The strict rhythm of the composition in this latter work does not in any way detract from the naturalness and dramatic mood of the entire scene.

The painter's popularity grew very quickly. With multitude of commissions, Rubens resorted to collaboration with his pupils and assistants, some of whom already were or later became leading artists—Anthony van Dyck, Jacob Jordaens, Frans Snyders, Jan Brueghel, called "Velvet Brueghel", among others. They absorbed Rubens' style and technique to the extent that it is sometimes difficult to distinguish the individual hands in the execution of a painting. The general idea of a work, however, its composition and colour range, were always Rubens' own, for he drew the first sketches and remained the creator, his assistants the executors. Their contribution was especially great between 1610 and 1620, though during this time Rubens often painted many entire pictures himself.

Rubens' artistic heritage is extremely varied. The scope of his interests is reflected in the wealth of subjects and their treatments, but even within this wide scope the moving force in his work was his inspired assertion of the grandeur, beauty, and unity of man and nature. This linked the painter with the humanistic traditions and lofty ethical ideals of the Renaissance. But Rubens was absolutely independent in his understanding of the beautiful and heroic. He proceeded less from traditional aesthetic conceptions or classical forms, than from direct observation of nature, simply emphasizing some of its features. Rubens' ideal of beauty embodied purely national and in some measure even popular conceptions of beauty, manly strength, and heroism. What attracts us in his images is not so much the conventional perfection of appearance or the refined nobility of proportions and forms, as their magnificent vitality and inexhaustible wealth of feeling.

Brought up in the ideals of humanism, throughout his life Rubens readily drew his subject matter from Greek and Roman mythology. The portrayal of the nude, in which Rubens, like many of his predecessors and contemporaries, expressed his notion of human beauty, was natural and customary in such subjects. One of his relatively early paintings, *Venus*

Portrait of Albert, the Artist's Son. 1616—18
Red and black chalks on paper,
eyelids touched with pen and ink;
11³/₄ × 8″ (30 × 20.5 cm)
The Hermitage, Leningrad

and Adonis (c. 1614, Hermitage, Leningrad; illustrated on jacket), shows us the artist's approach to mythological images. The plasticity of form, the sharp contours, and the thick brushwork and brilliant colours all heighten the glowing tones of the nude figures in this canvas, and generally characterize Rubens' style during this period.

His *Union of Earth and Water*, a masterpiece in the Hermitage that dates from about 1618, is a joyous hymn to mankind and to the mighty and eternal powers of nature. The painting is full of dynamism, despite its strict and orderly composition. The flowing movements of the figures are echoed by the folds of the draperies; the branches issue as if alive from the horn of plenty, drawn toward the heavens; water dashes in a mighty cascade from the urn, and waves dance lightly, splashing the gamboling putti. Movement, now strong and swift, now barely perceptible, pervades every detail of this picture and imbues it, as does the colour range, with the pulsating life so characteristic of Rubens' work. His compositions are never static. None of his contemporaries could match his free assurance in rendering the most complicated movements; his skill in uniting multifigured compositions into, as it were, one dynamic sweep; and, above all, his ability to express through movement the emotional intensity of his images.

These archetypical features of Rubens' art manifest themselves with particular force in his turbulent dramatic compositions, such as the *Battle of the Amazons* (1618—20, Alte Pinakothek, Munich), the so-called *Small Last Judgment* (1618—20, in the same museum), and in hunting scenes such as the *Lion Hunt* (1617—21, Alte Pinakothek, Munich; oil sketch in the Hermitage, Leningrad), where people and beasts swirl in the furious mass of a life-and-death struggle.

Rubens was able to combine in his religious paintings a profound solemnity of composition, triumphant richness of colour, and dramatic intensity of expression. Although the latter quality is sometimes very emphatic, these works do not seem forced or mannered because the artist's feeling is always sincere. A splendid example of a lively and dramatic interpretation of a New Testament theme is the *Feast in the House of Simon* (c. 1618, Hermitage, Leningrad).

The essence of Rubens' art and the representational element in his pictures remained constant throughout the master's life. But his artistic manner, his painterly technique, and his colour scale changed markedly over the years.

4

In many of the canvases he produced shortly before and after 1620, his quest for plastic expressiveness of form gives way to a more purely painterly treatment. Perceiving the world as an integral whole, Rubens does not isolate figures and objects from their actual surroundings, as he often does in his early works. A soft mist seems now to envelop the forms, blurring their contours and introducing a sense of air permeated with golden light. The artist's technique becomes freer and more flexible. In his colour schemes the juxtaposition of contrasting bright local colours is replaced by more integrated and harmonious coloristic patterns. He begins to favour saturated warm tones almost exclusively, working out their most complex nuances and relationships. All of these changes are apparent in one of his most fascinating paintings, *Perseus and Andromeda* (c. 1621, Hermitage, Leningrad). The poetic charm of this canvas lies in its faultless harmonious composition, its superb coloration, and the perfect rendition of the nude body, seemingly woven from the finest warm and cool tones. Everything in it praises natural beauty and strength. Glory crowns the brave hero who struck down the dragon; all around are romping putti; the powerful steed triumphantly raises his mighty wings. But the heroic aspect of the painting is softened by the lyrical feeling of love arising between Perseus and Andromeda, so that the warm glow enveloping the figure of the fair princess seems a reflection of the joyous agitation which fills her heart.

The beauty and valour of man is celebrated in the majority of Rubens' paintings. Hence he characteristically tends to create generalized types, though not infrequently endowing these with definite individual features. For much of his life commissioned portraiture was not Rubens' favourite genre, and we can presume that the sphere of portrait painting was rather limited to a master attracted by broader and more general ideological and artistic problems. But portraits constitute nonetheless an important part of Rubens' creative legacy and were among his first recognized masterpieces. In the *Equestrian Portrait of the Duke of Lerma* (1603, Prado, Madrid), and in a number of his early portraits of Genoese nobles, we see the first evidence of the Baroque style of portraiture which was eventually established in the work of Van Dyck. Later Rubens painted formal as well as intimate portraits, profoundly realistic and often extremely fine in characterization. The *Portrait of a Lady in Waiting to the Infanta Isabella* (c. 1625, Hermitage, Leningrad), one of the more intimate portraits, is full of feminine charm, and painted with unusual simplicity and lightness.

It is difficult to believe that the same artist was also the creator of imposing decorative cycles. Perhaps one of the most majestic of these is the cycle devoted to the life and reign of the French Queen Marie de' Medici (1622—25, now in the Louvre, Paris; oil sketch in the Hermitage, Leningrad). In keeping with the canons governing historical court painting at the time, Rubens combined in these pictures actual fact with allegory. He frequently introduced mythological and allegorical images, bringing them together with living people. The monumental nature of the compositions, the grandeur of the figures, their splendid attire, the opulence of the architectural and landscape background, the superb glowing colours, all combine to lend an incomparable decorative quality to these pictures which were produced with the extensive participation of the artist's workshop. Far more attractive are the oil sketches which Rubens painted himself, implementing his concepts with unsurpassed ease and spontaneity in a highly expressive and, it seems, definitive form. These sketches are remarkable for their free composition, daring technique, and the refined harmony of their colour scale.

Another major project, the decorations painted and erected in 1635 for the reception in Antwerp of their new Governor, the Cardinal-Infante Ferdinand, is known only from sketches and prints. Executed by Flemish artists after Rubens' designs, none of the triumphal arches, porticoes, and decorative walls survives today, but in his oil sketches we see that Rubens skilfully devised ever new compositional motifs and diverse sculptural and architectural forms. He did not limit himself to pure decoration, but imparted deeper meaning to these works. For example, in his composition *Mercury Departing from Antwerp* (Hermitage, Leningrad), Rubens seems to call on the new Governor to help the country overcome the loss of its former commercial importance; in the *Temple of Janus* he asks the ruler to put an end to the recent exhausting military operations on the borders of Flanders and Holland.

The 1630s were undoubtedly the most important period in Rubens' development, summing up of his art. To the end Rubens preserved his capacity to enjoy wholeheartedly the beauty of the surrounding world. A good example is *Bacchus* (between 1635 and 1640, Hermitage, Leningrad), a painting full of elemental, even ungovernable *joie de vivre*. In the last years of his life his pictures lost much of the decorative overloading that is typical of his earlier canvases; the realistic fabric of his work and his natural ties with the tradition of art in the Netherlands became especially tangible. During these years the master created only a few decorative paintings of large size, and the participation by members of his workshop became relatively less. More often Rubens painted for himself, following his own artistic predilections, independent of commissions. New themes reflecting the life of the common people began to attract his attention, as seen in *Kermess* (1635—36, Louvre, Paris) and *Peasants Dancing* (1636—40, Prado, Madrid). In his late portraits and landscapes, too, he creatively reinterpreted his lifelong impressions. It is difficult to overestimate the importance of these works in the context of the development of Western European painting. Rubens' heroic conception of the world is revealed in subjects taken from real life and rendered with unusual artistic perfection. In his landscapes, with their bold realistic treatment of space and light, Rubens constantly aimed at attaining an integral poetic image of the surrounding countryside. He tried to embrace the enormous wealth of nature in all its variety of form and emotion. Nature appears now peaceful and joyous, now full of stormy dynamism and tension, but always majestic and powerful. The figures populating these landscapes are not intended merely to enliven the picture, but are integral with the full-blooded life of the world. Such are the peasants walking along a road in *Peasants Returning from the Fields* (c. 1637, Pitti Gallery, Florence), and the shepherds in *Landscape with a Rainbow* (1632—35, Hermitage, Leningrad), in which Rubens achieves a striking emotional accord between man and nature.

His landscape sketches and studies are of a quite different, intimate character. Often very simple in subject matter, they illustrate the artist's power of observation and his keen, fresh approach to nature. Works of this kind, including the famous *Landscape with a Small Bridge* (1635—40, Hermitage, Leningrad), done in black chalk and gouache, should be considered to belong with the artist's graphic heritage. Rubens the draughtsman is no less great than Rubens the painter: the wide range of his interests and the diversity of the problems he solved are as fully revealed in his graphic art as in his painting.

Among Rubens' drawings, an important place belongs to the sketches and studies of human figures and especially to compositional sketches, often finished to the last detail. Of great interest are his numerous portrait and landscape drawings and animal pieces. Book illustrations and designs for architectural and sculptural compositions, too, have a place of their own in his art.

His technical range was very wide. He had perfect command of the techniques of pencil and pen-and-ink drawing. A born colourist, Rubens often introduced colour in his drawings by using tinted paper, pen and ink, watercolours, gouaches, chalks and pastels. His manner of drawing was extremely diverse; the changes it underwent over the years reflect the stages in his creative evolution. On the whole one

The Stoning of St. Stephen. 1617—18
Red and black chalks on paper with bistre
and watercolour washes and touches of pen and ink;
$18^{1}/_{2} \times 12^{3}/_{4}''$ (47 × 32.5 cm)
The Hermitage, Leningrad

can say that Rubens' painterly quality emerges more strongly in his later drawings. But his drawings from every period are distinguished by their free and impeccable execution. Form is generalized and laconic, conveyed with the temperament and improvization characteristic of his oil sketches. His graphic works preserve the monumental scope and breadth of his paintings while still displaying great refinement, often even elegance.

Rubens died in 1640 at the height of his creative powers and the peak of his fame, bequeathing to posterity not only an enormous artistic heritage, but also a brilliant school of painting. Thanks to him, Flanders played a leading part in the development of European art. And beyond the borders of his home country, Rubens' art and his undying glory was to inspire artists for many generations to come.

Vera Razdolskaya

BIOGRAPHICAL OUTLINE

1577   Born at Siegen (Germany) on June 28, to emigrant parents: Jan Rubens, a lawyer from Antwerp, and Maria Pypelinckx

1578—89   The family lives at Cologne

1587   Death of Jan Rubens, the artist's father

1589   The family returns to Antwerp

1591   Rubens studies under Tobias Verhaecht, landscape and decorative painter

1591—94   Attends the studio of Adam van Noort

1594—98   Completes his training under Otto van Veen

1598   Admitted to the Guild of St. Luke

1600—8   Lives in Italy as painter to Vincenzo Gonzaga, Duke of Mantua (Mantua, Florence, Venice, Genoa, and Rome)

1603—4   Trip to Madrid

1608   Returns from Rome to Antwerp

1609   Appointed court painter to the Household of the Archduke Albert and the Infanta Isabella, Governors of the Southern Netherlands in Brussels. Marries Isabella Brandt

1610   Purchases land in Antwerp for house and studio (completed 1615)

1621—27   Makes several trips to France to fulfil commissions at the French court, including the Marie de' Medici cycle (1622—25)

1626   Death of Isabella Brandt

1626—30   The main period of Rubens' diplomatic activity: trips to Holland; service in Spain and England. Numerous commissions for paintings at the Spanish and English courts

1630   Marries Hélène Fourment

1635   Acquires country estate, the Château of Steen, where he paints his late landscapes

1640   Dies in Antwerp on May 30

PLATES

THE DESCENT FROM THE CROSS. *c.* 1618
Oil on canvas. 99 × 66³/₄″ (297 × 200 cm)
The Hermitage, Leningrad

THE DESCENT FROM THE CROSS (detail)

STATUE OF CERES. 1612—15
Oil on panel. 35³/₄ × 25³/₄'' (91 × 65.5 cm)
The Hermitage, Leningrad

THE UNION OF EARTH AND WATER. *c.* 1618
Oil on canvas. 87^1/$_3$ × 71'' (222.5 × 180.5 cm)
The Hermitage, Leningrad

THE LION HUNT. Between 1617 and 1621
Oil on panel. 17 × 25¹/₄'' (43 × 64 cm)
Oil sketch for the picture in the Alte Pinakothek, Munich
The Hermitage, Leningrad

THE CARTERS. *c.* 1620
Oil on canvas (transferred from panel).
$34^1/_4 \times 49^3/_4''$ (87 $\times$ 126.5 cm)
The Hermitage, Leningrad

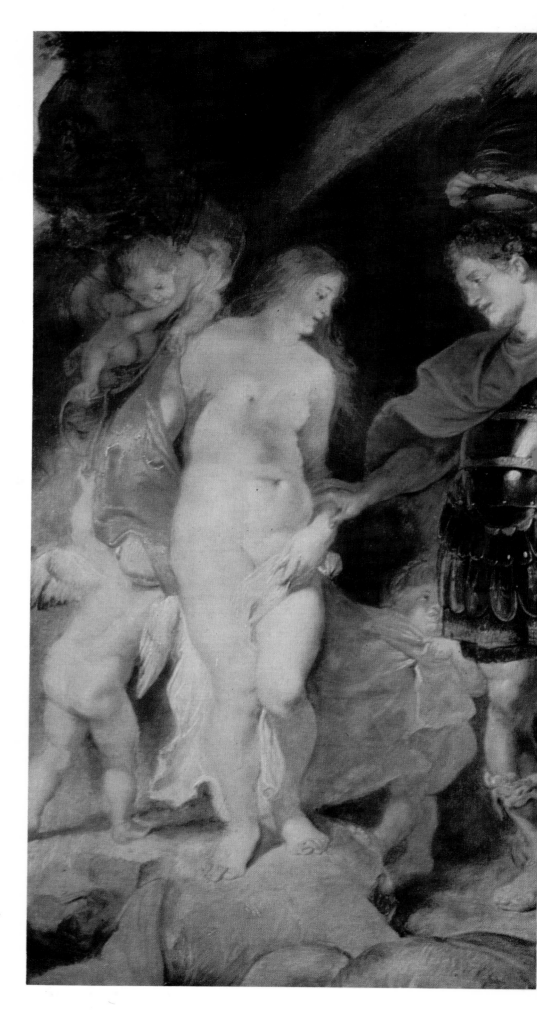

PERSEUS AND ANDROMEDA. *c.* 1621
Oil on canvas (transferred from panel).
39¹/₄ × 64³/₄'' (99.5 × 139 cm)
The Hermitage, Leningrad

PORTRAIT OF A LADY IN WAITING
TO THE INFANTA ISABELLA. *c.* 1625

Oil on panel. 25¹/₄ × 19″ (64 × 48 cm)
The Hermitage, Leningrad

THE CORONATION OF MARIE DE' MEDICI.
Between 1622 and 1625

Oil on panel. 19¹/₄ × 24¹/₂'' (49 × 63 cm)
Oil sketch for the picture in the cycle in the Louvre, Paris,
of *The Life of Marie de' Medici, Queen of France*
The Hermitage, Leningrad

THE CORONATION OF MARIE DE' MEDICI (detail)

MERCURY DEPARTING FROM ANTWERP. 1635

Oil on panel. 30 × 31'' (76 × 79 cm)
Oil sketch for a decorative structure honouring the arrival
of the new governor in Antwerp
The Hermitage, Leningrad

LANDSCAPE WITH A RAINBOW
1632—35

Oil on canvas (transferred from panel).
33¹/₄ × 51¹/₄″ (86 × 130 cm)
The Hermitage, Leningrad

BACCHUS. Between 1635 and 1640

Oil on canvas (transferred from panel).
75$^{1}/_{4}$ × 63$^{1}/_{2}$'' (191 × 161 cm)
The Hermitage, Leningrad

РУБЕНС

Альбом (на английском языке)
Издание третье

ИЗДАТЕЛЬСТВО „АВРОРА". ЛЕНИНГРАД. 1983
Изд. № 266. (1-40)
Типография имени Ивана Федорова, Ленинград
Printed and bound in the USSR